Cover Art

MW01167421

The cover art is modified from an 1879 painting by Bouguereau. It depicts Venus, "The Goddess of Love" born from out the shell. There has been much argument as to her being a Devil or a benevolent Goddess, depending on what she did for the receiving human. Sorrow and Joy, Tragedy and Comedy are all associated with acts of love. Without either the world would be barren of most books, plays, art, music, poetry, and all things imagined. This book of stories and poetry touches on some of these emotions that have lived in the hearts of so many, for so long.

j.f. sohn 04

Dedication

What else could I do but dedicate this book to all those loves remembered and those forgotten, either human or of nature that influenced me to write the thoughts and poetry found herein.

Dedication

Kathryn Wall and Art Cornell for the direction they provided for this, my first book.
Sansing McPherson for editing and review.
Aurora de Arce for art direction and encouragement.

Compliments

The following is a translation of part of a most complimentary, hand written letter that I received from a notable French friend. I had sent him an early self-published copy of my book "Foolish Heart".

He is Jean Beliard, a distinguished French Diplomat and friend of my family. He was a young French intelligence officer with Charles De Gaulle. He later became the French Ambassador to Canada, Mexico and Brazil as well as being Secretary of the "Atlantic Treaty Association" among other titles. He is now 86 years old and living beautifully with his wife just outside of Paris

He wrote in his letter of Oct. 11th, 2004

"Dear Sohn,

Yesterday the mail brought me this lovely surprise. My eyes have become "slow". I read 20 minutes at a time. But I could not leave your poems for hours. What talent ! as a writer and as a photographer. Thank you for thinking of me. Congratulations !

Jean"

Preface

As you travel through the stories and poems of this book you will find at times a change from my experiences to those of others. Some of these human events were told to me or transferred to me by some mystical messenger who found me to be an understanding and willing recipient. Others you will find to be both light and serious thoughts on life, love and people. Included is a story with a poem and loving thoughts that came out of a most romantic interlude resulting from sensitive internet communications. This is followed by my latest story and poem titled *"You Were Young"* It is a very emotional story and poem relating to a long ago deep love of mine in Paris. This past love is magically resurrected in thought and feeling by a visit from a younger lady in that magical city. In the back pages are poems relating to the beauty of nature and the universe and the emotional effect they have on our lives and our loves The last few pages are examples of the kind of art and poetry I combined and sent away every year as Christmas cards. Christmas, that time of year, when we are caught in thoughts of our childhood and the love and joy that Christmas brought to us all. If we were lucky.

For a deeper understanding of, and reason for the poem, the reader may find it more interesting to read the poem's *story* prior to the poem.

Foolish Heart - story

It was 1980 – The breakup of my second marriage. My wife was an award winning watercolor artist. I loved her work and she loved mine as an architect. We traveled joyously together through-out Europe and America without any discord. I had believed that this love would last forever. We were extremely compatible and enjoyed the beauty of all things created by man and nature. We relocated to Hilton Head Island in South Carolina. All seemed perfect until I discovered her to be unfaithful. I was more than deeply hurt. I, like King Arthur, had lost a dream. Camelot was no more. Hearing "Misty watercolor memories of the way we were" was just more salt on the wound. This poem was written to remind me to not rush into a new love that was not first based on friendship. It is a shame that both women and men do not easily recognize the value of developing a very good friendship prior to sex. So many potentially good and lasting loves have been destroyed by rushing into the bedroom much too soon. Friendship and Patience, I now believe, are the glue for maintaining the early love of your potential soul mate. Later when your hearts soundly tell you that you are now ready to cross over into a committed love, it will be the greatest physical love that is ever experienced between two lovers. Save it for that moment.

Foolish Heart

Oh foolish heart, don't tempt me so

To love again, although I know

To be alive, with joy of heart

To dream and plan another start

I have to love, I have to care

With someone close, I need to share

And though I know so deep within

The joy that love alone can bring

I fear that love and dread the pain

Of being hurt and lost again

So foolish heart, this time be kind

And don't beat too strong, until I find

The one who first a friend can be

Who later falls in love with me

j.f. sohn 1982

A Prayer To The Heart - story

Though I hoped that my heart would protect me from tempting new loves, there were times when I let myself stray. I foolishly believed that I was then able to protect myself, but I was not sure. I was getting some of those old loving feelings again and that scared me. At that point, in a prayer to my heart, I asked again for wisdom and guidance and I put my fate in its care. I hope that there will be a time when my heart will recognize a matching heart that will be lasting and I will no longer need help. I will then be free to love again with the joy of endearing passion and without fear. What a wonderful thing that would be.

Dear foolish heart, forgive me,
for I have taken a step into
that unknown land of potential
hurt and pain that I asked
you to protect me from.
Have I done this with your
blessing because you have
recognized another heart that
has been hurt like mine?
Does that other heart also yearn
for a love that has been denied?
Teach me to again be loving
and tender and keep me from ever
causing hurt to a wounded heart.
Let me again live with the joy that
only comes from two loving
hearts that beat as one.
Do this and I will need little else.

Amen

A difficult love story

When you meet a lovely too-young lady during the separation time of your divorce, you are in trouble. Especially if she shows and expresses a desire for you. You are beat down, feeling that you have failed and life has no desirable future. Now her spirit and vitality are like an Elixir She makes you forget your unhappiness. She brings life to your soul and you want more. You experience desire again and it is fulfilled. You are in a trance; a fantasy perfect for you. Then after a while, reality returns and you see her in a different light. Her playful spirit has immaturity. Her logic and reality is lost in a dream world. She wants to escape her environment and believes that you will be able to provide her way out. You confront her and she has a tantrum. You tell her that you love her but that there is no future in the relationship. You didn't want to hurt her or anyone, but it was one of those unfortunate realities of life. Now you are lost again; you don't know what to do other than to walk away. You do and she is deeply hurt and so are you.

Conundrum

Fantasy is the medication for Reality

Reality is the antitoxin for Fantasy

j.f. sohn 82

How We Were

I sit too much and think of her
of how we loved and how we were
The holding hands, the walks alone
Those times together in her home
Her funny dog, she loved to hold
and tease, chase and even scold
We danced, we laughed, we talked of love
and serious things like God above
Our past, our sins, our hopes, our dreams
but now how strange this whole thing seems
For we are not together

Is life a game, a test, a trial
my love for her I've no denial
And yet I hesitate to speak
desire strong but courage weak
What is it that I really seek
since we are not together

I don't know where to go from here
I want her still but now I fear
That reality will fade away
And fantasy will win the day

I hurt, I cry, I curse the pain
I even prayed to God in vain, that
somehow all of this would change

Well- perhaps in time the hurt will
pass so we can talk or even laugh
at life and things that made us do
the foolish things that lovers do

She - story

She, is the story of a scattered and confusing romance with a lovely young lady of many faces and moods. I met her in church during the time that I was still trying to recover from my divorce. It was not always easy to be with her. You never knew what she was going to do, leave you, kiss you or undress you, but under all those mixed feeling she was at times wonderfully tender and warm. She presented me with my first bible. I still have it as a kind remembrance.

A relating thought

Like shells upon the sand
And women still at hand
Most pretty ones are broken

j.f. sohn

She

She laughs, she's cutting,
she's sharp, and she's fast
She can hurt you deeply
and she can make it last
She can make you love
and she can make you cry
She can make you mad
and she can make you lie
She is ravishingly crude,
gutsy and loud,
Silently lonely,
but a charm in a crowd.
She's a child lost
a girl and a boy
Erratic, volcanic,
a clown and a joy
She snaps, she breaks
falls apart at the seams
She cries, she prays and goes
on with her dreams
She's a beauty of face
and a beauty within
She has much love to give
but not as a sin
She's my silent love
my conscience, my thorn
She may now treat me cool
but she still leaves me warm.

j.f. sohn 1982

The Sage Of Time - story

Every once in a while you experience a kiss from a young lady that is so warm and loving, that you don't want it to stop. You want to go further. Then reality steps in and you return to past lessons learned. You both have been drinking and you don't want to take advantage of the moment. With difficulty you break away and leave. Then?

The Sage Of Time

I thought I had the sage of time
and lessons of past loves to guard me
but as sudden as the morning mist
her parting kiss disarmed me
lips apart, so soft and moist
bodies warm and wanting
How wonderful that moment was
with feelings deep and taunting
I yearned for more but feared to stay
with wine it's so deceiving
So I said good night and walked away
and now regret my leaving

j.f. sohn 1982

Tomorrow - story

In my professional and social life I got to know many of the personal stories of the wives of the kind of men who could afford me as well as their wanting wives. This poem sadly reflects the feelings of many of these ladies. It also at times can equally apply to men of socially active or business involved wives.

Tomorrow

I hoped I dreamed I waited long
For time from you to borrow
But the promises you gave to me
Were always for tomorrow

I've lost the hope I've lost the dream
No more thoughts of time to borrow
You're caught within your corporate world
And you'll still be there tomorrow

j.f. sohn 1985

Games of Love - story

I was living in New York and was invited by a friend to attend a black tie "Bachelor Party" given by an elegant lady of means. It was a party like you would find depicted in a movie. Elegant, with many lovely smiling ladies and many aggressive smiling men with calling cards. The next day I did the gentlemanly thing and called to thank the lady who had given the party. This led to a conversation on the subject of the relationships of supposedly more mature adults. A subject she was well versed in. Her humor and tragedy on the games that people still play as adults, led to this poem.

Games of Love

It seemed so logical to me
That games of love should cease to be
When life achieves maturity
But oh how wrong this logic be
For it's so plain to see
That lessons learned of life do flee
When cupid's bow doth conquer thee

What need between two lovers still
To tease the heart and mind to fill
With anxious moments waiting long
To see a sign or hear the song
That sets your heart to sing

Oh God - why doesn't the telephone ring ?

j.f. sohn 1985

13

Unrequited Love

Dreams & I Have A Love - story

I don't really care to remember the desperate feelings we get when we don't receive the response we wish from the person of our dreams. It is a deeply hurtful yearning that we can't seem to overcome. All we can do is hope for the miracle of a loving and positive response from that person. Life is so strange in the way that it causes us to be highly attracted to someone who is a challenge, and we ignore the ones who are too easy. For some reason I had three poems that covered this dilemma.

Fate

In matters of love
what sadder thing be true
Than to find what you were looking for
wasn't looking for you
j.f. sohn 84

Dreams

Oh what beautiful dreams I dream
Together you and me
And oh how I cherish those loving
dreams and yearn for their reality
And oh how I suffer the painful
thoughts that they will never be
Give me a light- some hope- a sign
that my dreams are also yours
And in spite of all the dragon's fire
and castle walls so high
We'll learn to live and love as one
Forever till we bye

I have a love

I have a love who has no love for me
No chance have I to see her and touch her
Only her picture to lay beside me
Oh why can't I lose this unceasing obsession
Why can't I love the one's who love me
Too long have I waited, wishing and dreaming
That somehow her love would come now to me
But time has not blessed me with all of my wishes
My dreams are still dreams and my fate
yet to be
So what can I do to end this dilemma
I need her beside me or I need to be free
No answer from logic, no help from above
I'm trapped in my folly, and helpless in love
j.f. sohn 4/11/86

Dear Susan - story

Long Island, New York, 1986. I met a lively and cute young lady at one of Long Island's better Disco Night Clubs. Afterwards we had a couple of fun dates when she asked me if I would please fax a message to her at her office. Perhaps I had recited a couple of my poems to her and she was expecting something cute and original or maybe she just wanted for some reason to show-off to the office gang. I don't know, but anyway I agreed. Obviously her name was Susan and therefore "Dear Susan".

Dear Susan,

This fax you'll find a bit bizarre
but that's what happens - when you are
requested by a damsel fair to communicate
in faxened flair
So I will try and now will say in this
bemused communiqué'
Greetings my sweet Susan
in the middle of the day
Of course I must reserve my thoughts
and careful what I say
For staff and friends are also there
in the middle of the day
Should I tease or even try
to be a little flirty
maybe yes or maybe no
But - by all means don't be dirty

With sweetest thoughts I'll also try
for these can come with easing
Remembering the day we met
and our evening - oh so pleasing
I hope the future will persist
to treat us just as kind
So we can be together long
and further friendship find
There are so many things to see
and places we can go
So many thoughts and dreams to share
so much yet to know
So many jokes I've yet to tell
and hope that you'll find funny
So many little things to buy
providing there's the money
Thinking of that I must get back
to business and my duty
To serious work and client's needs
instead of you - my beauty
In final thought and in humor play
I never thought that I would say
Oh Susan
I certainly enjoyed faxing you
in the middle of the day

j.f. sohn 1986

Unbound Love - story

This is a poem of remembrance of a deep passionate love I had for an extremely beautiful, intelligent and cultured lady with high morals and ethics. A former Miss New York. She was quite a change relative to what I had experienced in my prior years. We shared our love for several years. She wanted to get married and have children. That was something I neither could do or wanted to do at that time. I had to return to Hilton Head on very personal family matters. She wanted to stay near her parents in New York. We are still very good friends but I always have wished that life had arranged things differently for us. I keep her photo on a shelf beside me and still think of her every day. I wish that we could have gone to Paris together.

Unbound Love

I miss her so, although I know
our love can never be
And memories last of our passions past
that haunt me constantly

What game these gods do play with me
to tease my fragile heart
With precious tastes of love and joy
that all too soon depart

Once more I want to hold her near
and feel her bosom swell
With each and every panting breath
that's quickened by the spell
Of touching hands and touching lips
exploring every turn

So softly met, so lightly felt
in slowly mounting burn
Of passion's fire and love's desire
that's rarely ever found
Except with loves that never find
a way of being bound

J.F.Sohn

Fantasy - story

This experience was one of those once in a lifetime happenings which is usually accompanied with the expression WOW or in French Oh Lá Lá. Just back on the Island from a few years in New York I went to a Chamber Of Commerce social. It was there that I saw my WOW. Not only did I see her but she saw me (the old eyes across the room scenario). She took my arm and led me to the bar where we had drinks and exchanged life stories. This WOW had class and a lot of creative energy. Oh boy I said to myself, Foolish Heart, watch yourself, this highly desirable Goddess of love could be dangerous. This one however didn't get dangerous but became a very long lasting, close and faithful friend. A rare item these days.

Tomorrows

The Gods graced our lives
At a special moment in time
May our tomorrows together
Be forever as beautiful
As the beginning

j.f. sohn

Fantasy

I met a dream, A joy surreal

A fantasy of love

I now again have found that heart

I once was absent of

But fantasies I know to be

So lost in life's reality

So slowly go, oh beating heart

And chills that run my spine

Until the day, when I can say

in words so true divine

She is real - she is real - and she is mine

j.f. sohn © 1993

Butterfly - story

This is a poem written specifically for The WOW lady in Fantasy. It tells a story of the unfortunate thoughts that many men, including myself have upon seeing a beautiful, vibrant and outgoing blond with a well developed figure. Beyond the bar at the Chamber social this is the true picture of that fabulous woman that I kept as a friend, because I was afraid to lose her as a lover

Butterfly

Her spirit danced in morning light
So beautiful, delicate, so colorfully bright
She pleased my senses and pleased my eye
But only as a butterfly
That lands upon extended hand
With innocence and trust in man
I knew her not beyond that view
Nor did I care at first to do

Then suddenly one quiet night
That butterfly in silent flight
Evolved again in what did seem
A metamorphosis beyond a dream

What once I knew as pure delight
An amusement sought to please the night
Became a woman real, who cast a spell
Like Venus born from out the shell

She knew of warmth and love and pain
Creative moods, artistic reign
She bubbled forth in thought and verse
With charm and heart she did immerse
In tales of life both sad and gay
That caused me shame and thought to say

How dare we men to think so base
Of womankind, that God did grace
With beauty rare in form and face
That we ignore or chance deny
Her beauty is more than, just a butterfly

j.f. sohn 93

23

While visiting a fine art gallery in Atlanta, I met this beautiful and charming young lady who was the assistant manager. We easily found a great common interest in truly discussing art without further thoughts or maneuvers on my part. I strangely can't remember how our involvement progressed from there to becoming lovers but I won't try because it was evidently something we both needed at that moment in time. This timely romantic interlude was heart warmingly enhanced one night at a local Hilton Head disco where we danced with each other till near closing. Surprising to me, we were really wonderful together on the dance floor and as with lovers, perfect moves and timing. That was the last time I really enjoyed dancing. It's funny how a simple thing like beautifully dancing together can bond you to someone. I continue to remember that evening in all ways. She later met a wealthy gentleman from Connecticut and married him. Maybe he too danced well with her. C'est la vie.

I Think Of You

As morning light retreats the night
in radiant hues of colors bright - I think of you
As singing birds begin the day
before they kiss and fly away - I think of you
As scent of tea awakens me from lovely
dreams of things to be - I think of you
As every hour that fills the day
and passes by in sweet array - I think of you
With inner sense of feelings soft, your touch,
your skin, your thoughts aloft - I think of you
With memories left of dinners fine, of music
sweet and sparkling wine - I think of you
With tender passion and childish fun in warm
embrace, we two as one - I think of you
The fun filled time we danced till two
With pleasure now - I think of you

In silent sleep throughout the night with only
dreams to make it right - I think of you
And so begins another day - another time
And chance to say - I think of you

j.f. sohn 1994

Passions Warm - story

This poem was written for a beautiful lady from Spain, who had recently moved to Florida. I had contacted her through, an internet service to be a dinner companion with me and my friends when I came to visit them in Miami. In the process of our e-mail letters and before we actually met, we became quite close. We had very compatible backgrounds and interests. She knew of the arts and design. She grew up in a family of ambassadors and diplomats. She had class and elegance, spoke superb English as well as French and Italian. She was a sensitively romantic and yet very humorous lady. We exchanged jokes as well as serious love stories of our lives. It amazed me how close two people can get by simple word communications and photo exchanges. One of these "close" nights, she indicated that she was going off to bed. I said "Take me with you in your dreams". With this great lead for a poem I immediately sat down and wrote "Passions Warm". and e-mailed it to her. She was passionately taken by it and when we later met it open the doors for a beautiful, warm and loving interlude. Our emotions were in perfect balance. Through our written and verbal communications we became very good friends before we became lovers. We have maintained this loving relationship ever since.

Passions Warm

Take me with you in your dreams and
let the night explore
Each and every passion deep that makes
you cry for more.

Let its passing slowly drift through
every secret thought
Of every kind of love you sought but
never ever caught

If then in life we cause to meet and
something deep within
Tells us each to take a chance, then
let the games begin

And may our future nights to be
all we could desire
A lover kind with passions warm,
that never seem to tire.

j.f. sohn

E-mail Lovers
Love Poem

My dearest - You truly on this day
are my one and only Valentine love.
Be it imaginary, be it foolish, be it only
in my heart and mind,
Be it only that I have cast you as today's
leading lady in my surreal play of divine joy.
It is you, really you, no one else.
On this day and if for no more than it,
take me with you in your thoughts.
Feel me warmly in your heart, and let these
thoughts stimulate every forgotten emotion
that only comes from that
spiritual union of two needing loves.

j.f. sohn 03

Saint Valentine's Day - Laments

Dearest love, what am I to think when the lady of my heart is out there with
someone else on St. Valentine's Day evening. Not knowing what new frog may
have captured your fragile heart and had taken you to a momentary frog heaven
for a one nighter on his frogcycle. If not that, then a reasonable scenario would
be that such a beautiful maiden as you would surely have been pursued by many
a noble or not so noble knight who wished to carry the delicate silk panties of his
lady on the tip of his lance as he rides triumphantly back and forth before the
cheering crowd. Another conquest for Sir Bragsalot.

Oh what scenes of life's futile efforts at love I can conceive that are practiced
throughout the world on this day and oh what wondrous lucky few who are given
the secret Elixir.

Letter to a buddy about Valentine's Day

I sir, spent a most delightful and loving Valentine's Day at my computer writing romantic words and poems to my beautiful, delightful and inspiring lady from Spain. Just think of the money I saved by this simple modern method of romancing and flattering a beautiful sexy lady. No flowers or candy, no expensive dinners or presents, no lavish suite at a deluxe love nest that you prepaid, just in case. No concern as to how I looked or dressed, no need to buy breath mints or little blue pills. Just my words were enough to make her extremely happy and excited. She of course reciprocated with her own wonderful words and compliments as well as aspirations of a loving and sensuous rendezvous at some time in the future. What more could men of our age want on Valentine's Day. Oui - je sait. I can think of something else too. I don't need your help for that. But I can say from experience that sometimes that subject is often more satisfying in the mind and in the anticipation than in reality. And thank God, you need not have to say, gee, I'm sorry, that never happened before. I must have had too much to drink. Better - Yes?

Image

My dearest love, how tender your words of love as I hide here behind my computer and write words you may believe are of a different man. Would that I could be that man, would that you could love me as you love the image that is in your heart.

Prayer for a Lady

Before I lay me down to sleep,
I pray for a lady who's worthy to keep.
One who is lovely, smart and serene,
One who can listen and never be mean.
One who will call before I'm asleep,
Is reasonably rich and keeps herself lean.
Scratches my back and make
love in all ways. Is gentle and fun
as she cuddles and plays.
I pray that this lady will
love me no end, always be true
and always a friend.
But why need I pray, for
now I can say, with her photo
beside me as I lie in my bed,
Never mind God - I've found her.
Amen.

Being With You

Dearest love, after all our serious talk I can still say things that I have left out as to my thoughts of us together. You give me feelings that we could do such out of character childish things together. Like jumping and rolling around in a hay loft, running through and hiding in a cornfield, jumping and splashing in the ocean waves, racing at waters edge, scaring the sandpipers and gulls, eating a sloppy chili dog, making funny noises and faces, giggling in bed, singing together in the shower, making funny designs on dishes with left over food then looking into each other's eyes and saying - my God but I love being with you.

Upon Receiving a Bathing Suit Photo

My God Venus - What did you do with the shell? I believe that if I were to be with you now and if I were to see your beauty before me I would need many a moment, just to view you as a magnificent work of art. I would have to stand back restraining my every desire and spend those moments absorbing every inch and curve of your alabaster beauty. Then in my mind I would create a melodious magic garden within which we could be with each other alone, slowly touching and absorb from each those incredible sensual expressions that we have been wanting to pour forth for such a long long time.

She asked "What do I want in a woman"

Oh you sweet innocent love, I could be present- culture crude and tell you what the typical male would say. But I believe that the implication is understood. Now if we go by my culture level – My dear all you have to do is name all of the qualities that you have so well expressed or demonstrated in the multitude of writings that we have exchanged and that is exactly what I want in "My" woman. And that is the dilemma - Where could I ever find another like you - I have been with soooo many women in the past several years and no one has approached your simple beautiful qualities. All I was presently looking for was someone as a dinner companion and I got my dream of a lifetime. Now what Gods are playing games with me to see how I work this one out.

Misty Moon - story

It was a late evening on Hilton Head. The moon was full but misted out at times by passing clouds. I was sitting in my friend's car listening to him lament his recent break-up with his wife. A subject I could well relate to. The moon roof of his car was open. I looked up and poetically said " A misty moon I see above". That's all I needed to be awakened at night to write without pause the poem *"Misty Moon"*. I wrote it for him but it applies as well to so many of us.

Misty Moon

A misty moon I see above
Through misty eyes without my love
Do you as I oh misty moon
Regret a love you lost too soon
In sadness now I think of mine
And all her childish charms
Remembered nights in warm embrace
Within her loving arms
All cuddled up in tender hold
Without a sound, till whispers told

I Love You, I Always Will

Then sleep would come
And all was still
We all have known these precious nights
With lovers wrong or lovers right
When innocence in spell so cast
That we believed our love would last
Well now for me that love is bye
Another dream another try
So misty moon now bid me well
In silent passing of your spell
With hope the pain I feel tonight
Will leave me free by morning light

j.f. sohn © 1994

33

Find Me A Lover - story

I was driving through South and North Carolina on my way back to New York. I was listening to about the only thing available on the radio in that area, "Country Music" or whatever they call it. The subjects seemed to dwell mostly on lost loves or other dramatic love situations. I said to myself, hell I've been there, I should be able to write one of my own. At first I did it as though I were reciting it in a southern or western accent. Kind of making fun. Then one day I looked at it and realized that what I had written was a really touching poetic story that is not unique to just country western. It could have at one time been anyone of us.

Find Me A Lover

So sad is this story I'm telling you of
I've had many lovers, but none I could love
Oh, so many lies to make them feel fine
So many love songs, but none of them mine
For sure I gave all you could ever think of
To all of those lovers I never could love
That is, all except one thing, that's sure
to be told
No warmth from my heart, would ever unfold
I've grown oh so weary, free, but alone
I yearn now for something, I use to call home
So I look to the stars, and I pray up above
Oh Lord, God please, find me a lover
I really, really - can - love

j.f. sohn 1990

When an older man is single, eligible, attractive, looks reasonably healthy and prosperous and of course has a fine sense of humor the curiosity of women, single or married, gets the best of them. They just have to ask. "What are you looking for in a woman." They can't believe that he could be quite happy without one. Especially if he has been previously spoiled by a much better menu or has highly suffered from a selection from that menu. Then of course is the thought that maybe he is gay. This sometimes causes the man to prove his manhood and this usually gets him quickly classified as a horny beast. He can't win. Best he should be prepared with a good story that might still give him an escape route. The following poem attacks this human issue.

Too often I am asked, by someone
oh so curious
"What is it that you really want"
"What is it you are seeking"?
My answer calm without a thought
of being too injurious
I seek not now a soul-mate,
be her simple or with class
A love affair is not my want
On this I'll surely pass
I revel in the simple joys only
friendships can imbue
Without the kind of stupid things,
that lovers surely do
I need the warmth of laughter
and just a hug or two
A kiss upon her rosy cheek,
a twinkle in her eye
A smile across her lovely face
with lips of sprinkled dew
A hand that's warm while holding
mine as we just walk along
Without a single thought of things
that ever would be wrong
This lass I fear is hard to be,
a thought that is endearing
I wonder if she really were,
could I resist her ever being
And though I say so boldly,
for love I'm not now seeking
Would I be so false a man
if I tried a little peeking?

j.f. sohn 2003

Paris, March 17, 2004 - An hotel near Charles de Gaulle airport. I had a layover to catch a following day's flight back to the States. While having a light lunch in the bar area a most attractive and beautifully proportioned lady walked up to the bar and also ordered a lunch. She was elegantly dressed in black leather boots, tight black leather pants, a black shirt under a designer black leather jacket. She wasn't wearing any makeup but her lovely blond hair was beautifully coifed. I would describe her as a Sharon Stone without make up. She turned looking for a place to sit. I of course got up and asked her to join me. She accepted and there began an hour of delightful and humorous conversation. I learned that she was an American and a pilot for a commercial air carrier. An ageless beauty, never married, had an apartment in Paris and had many other very interesting side interests. Needless to say I found her to be an extremely interesting and desirable lady. What a wonderful gift of the Gods on a boring afternoon in a strange hotel. On departing for her assigned flight she gave me a way to contact her. This was encouraging and flattering. That evening in my room, I thought things about flying over ancient and mystic lands that I had never thought of before. Do we ever think of all the history that has occurred over the lands below as we fly by. The drama of these and the loves and wars occurring then are haunting. I wrote the following poem to her in which I tried to express these complex thoughts in a digested and simple manner. She received the poem which she understood and she was highly touched by its symbolism.

Angel In The Sky

Dearest angel in the sky,
flying off o'er Paris high
O'er ancient lands with histories
past and mystic tales that dreams
did cast, from out the minds
of gods and men, to be inscribed
by willing pen
Loves and wars once brought
to end do start again and
death does flow as now you
scan the earth below.
How wonderful, to be above,
where beauty cures this
saddened plight, above the
clouds, in billowed white
Peace by day and peace by night
How now it is for me to see,
this ever tranquil, place to be

j.f. sohn 3/17/04

Magic Dreams - story

Remember the 80s?; when discos existed everywhere and were crowded with wild young people and loud wild music. They try to look like they are having fun, dancing, drinking, flirting and hoping desperately to meet their future love. For those who can't get into the discos the shopping malls become a different chance for more searching, flirting and new adventures. Behind all this is the reality of young people hoping to find someone to take them away from their unhappy lives, they want to live the magic dream that they see in films or that they read about in romance novels or in magazines. "Magic Dreams" tries to tell this story along with a way-out for those who have lost hope of achieving their dream.

Magic Dreams

So many lives looking for magic
searching through the eyes
So many lives wishing and dreaming
behind a cheerful disguise
They scan the malls and disco halls
in search of that magic glance
From someone who is looking too
to take a magic chance
So many lives with empty hearts
looking for that magic dream
The perfect love, the perfect mate
that hope of life supreme
But who am I to mock the spell
of magic and it's charms
For life I've seen in absent dreams
and learned to fear her harms
We need to look for magic wands
and think our magic thoughts
We need to fantasize our lives
and lose what truth has brought
Reality we learn is filled
with painful sparks of fire
But the magic thoughts and dreams
we dare will soon our hearts inspire
So listen all you young and old
who lost your wills desire
To fight another battle born
of life's relentless mire
Partake of magic thoughts and dreams
and build your castles high
So you can see beyond the walls
to other lands you'll try
For there you'll find another chance
to start your life anew
And search again for those magic eyes
that only search for you

j.f. sohn 1984

Leisure Time - story

I met a fairly attractive but aging lady of means, who was rather bored with her life on the Island. This life for her then became an endless sequence of booking cruises to anywhere she thought might relieve her plight. I don't believe that she ever will succeed because she lacked the ability to see the immediate beauty around her. She had little in creative thoughts and I had no sympathy for her. There are so many useful things to be done for those less fortunate. One evening she called, wanting me to come to her. She sounded as if she had had a few drinks. She said the words "The day is gone and it is dark" etc. etc.. I wished her well, went to my desk and e-mailed her the following poetic note. She never called me again. Lucky me.

Leisure Time

The day is gone and it is dark
How quick the hours did embark
On needless thoughts and wasted wine
Your life adrift in leisure time
That earns you naught a single thought
Of life that is fulfilling

j.f. sohn 2004

Forgive Me - story

In spite of the drama that is expressed in this poem that I wrote, I have absolutely no recollection of who it was meant for. So in case there is a lady out there who deserves it from me and never got it then she can take pleasure in thinking it was for her.

Forgive Me

Forgive me please for loving you
and being such a pain
Forgive my acts, forgive my calls,
forgive this old refrain
Oh why did life repose on me
this love I cannot shed
From day to day and year to year,
with no one else instead
I know not how to ease this need
I have of loving you
And I often pray for the miracle
of another love as true
So until the day, when I do find,
that love with someone new
My endearing thoughts of
happiness can only be of you

j.f. sohn

Love Is Not Forever - story

Being single again, I was told a lot of stories of other people's failures in marriage. These were stories from what I found to be nice people, both from the women as well as the men. This bothered me and I was driven to write a poem that might encourage these and other people to try a little harder. It's not a great poem but it does touch on things that are needed to stay in love, or at least stay married until phase two of love is discovered. I read this poem at a friend's wedding. His second. The new marriage broke up after one year. So much for instructive poetry.

Pure Love

Shared between two lovers
Pure love can do no wrong
Pure love is the light of heaven
Pure love is natures song

j.f. sohn

Love Is Not Forever

Love is not forever, even when it's true
Love is not forever, except for just a few
So treasure every moment, while love
is in your heart
And cherish every pleasure that love
alone can start
Share your dreams together,
fly off to the moon
Leave the world behind you,
for time is lost so soon
Don't promise for tomorrow,
live out every day
Only think of giving and maybe
love will stay
Look for all the beauty
You each do have within
Encourage every effort, don't think
what might have been
Don't run when time is troubled
don't cheat when you're away
Don't want for any other and
maybe love will stay
Now - in spite of all the hurt
that life is sure to bring
The jealousies, the loss of faith,
that "innocent little fling"
Talk out all your feelings listen
close and pray
That you can still forgive the faults
and maybe love will stay
What happens after this is
really left to you
I only know as I have said and
you should all know too
That, Love is not forever, even when it's true
Love is not forever except for - *just a very few*
j.f. sohn 1981

Above are images of Paris, the romantic city of my birth and the setting of a long ago beautiful and emotional "Grand Amour". Since the influence of that romantic city and the incredible beauty of the lady of that time, I was never able to escape the constant memories of those special moments in my early life. Then one day those memories and loving feelings were surprisingly reawakened by a visit from a lovely young lady in that magic city. We had been past friends but not in Paris. The story of this touching romance between two lovers of different ages, caught in the influence of the beauty and romance of Paris is expressed in the poem "You Were Young".

Paris as a setting for any deep romance will transcend age and will elevate that love to its highest emotion. The memory of those feelings will forever haunt you and influence you as you travel on through life and other loves. I believe that it is this romantic background that has influenced and directed my thoughts and writings.

You Were Young

You were young, and I was past
the age of lightness in my path
Yet you did cause my heart to sing
as youth in love at time of spring
when all is beauty, all is gay,
the birds do sing, the children play
Was I so then afraid to show
my feelings deep, the inner glow
that you did cause, yet little know
how you did start a mental flow
of lost desires, once asleep, now
kindled bright again for me
to dream of things that use to be
Is it too late, am I too old to seek
again a youthful goal of joyous days
with you so sweet with heart of gold,
who held my hand as we did stroll
along the streets of Paris old
Though it windy - though it cold,
with you beside me did unfold
a warmth within, once only told
in tales of love and passions deep,
that only youth was meant to keep
Now here am I in silent thought of
love and kindness that you brought,
to me, a man now past the age of
wanting thoughts of warm caresses,
touching skin, a driving force
still live within
Is it so much a mortal sin, to once
again desire these, the fruits of youth,
the things that please
To lust and want as only known
to passioned men of younger tone

cont.

47

Could there emerge a love from you,
blind of age, blind of stories
to be told, of lovers born of different
times, different lives, different mores
Feeding strong on what we shared,
things of beauty things of fun
regardless of and unaware of all
but what we were as one
What a dream, what desire,
what a miracle it would require
Yet I wish this dream to be,
me with you - you with me
What kind of man that I now be,
to wish for things of fantasy
Life is real and often cruel, am
I a dreamer or a fool to think
that I could bend the rule
So dearest love, my lady fair, with
charm and heart can you now
bear these thoughts of mine, because
of you, be them foolish or be them true
This I write as now I feel,
I miss you deeply, emotions real
They all may pass, they all may go,
like autumn leaves before the snow
But at this moment, I can say,
my thoughts of you live every day
and I wish you near me every night,
be it wrong or be it right
I ask no answer, ask no say,
neither now or any day
Just think of me with fondest heart,
though we now are far apart
A lover past, a friend to last
Romantic times that life did cast
upon us once at time of need
An act of God that plants the seed
of love and caring shared by two
You for me - Me for you
Bonsoir my love – Jacques Paris Feb. 2004

STUDIO ÉLYSÉES
PARIS

Remembrance of Paris - Long ago

Biki - Fashion model - Elle cover girl
Daughter of a French Baron
A fun companion and love

Wrapped in her cloak of silent beauty
She cruised the hearts of men

Many words have been written by many in an attempt to say what happens when you experience the best of anything in life. The universal conclusion seems to be that it is near impossible afterwards, to accept anything less.

My early beautiful life and love in Paris seems to have left me in this unfortunate state. Sensing this malady, I wrote myself the following question along with my final self analysis.

Oh, why do I so quickly go
From one love to another
What fantasies are in my mind
What new could I discover
I have a need and yet I fear
That nothing new will ever
Fill that need I have within
In spite of my endeavor.

Paris - 2004

Unbound Love

Paris - Long Ago

Once Upon a Time

Love and Pain

So many have said that the pain will not last
That time will dissolve all the hurt that is cast

So what is the purpose for all of the pain
What is the lesson what is the gain

Is it destined by nature is it part of a plan
That's fated to touch every woman and man

A game by the Gods they thought to derive
To test our strength and will to survive

Are we better for trying although we have lost
Are we stronger and wiser in spite of the cost

Is it life's human callus for the hurt yet ahead
A kind of protector, a shield in good stead

Then, regret not the loves that failed here to stay
And gain from the pain that came by the way

Be patient and calm, hold on to your pride
Don't shy from new loves but hold them aside

Perhaps then in time and with faith you can be
Better to love and once again free

j.f. sohn - 11/94

52

Wife

We met and loved together
With passion and desire
We learned about each other
Explored our inner fire

We cuddled oh so warmly
Held hands and touched with love
Embraced that love between us
Gave thanks to God above

We dreamed and planned together
The tomorrows we would share
With children born of wanting
And friendships formed with care

We cheered through all the good times
Shared pain through all the bad
Sweat the anxious moments
Struggled through the sad

So why has life so changed us
We did what we thought right
Followed all conventions
Prayed near every night

Is this the way it's meant to be
With passing of the time
Do passions die, does love depart
Is she no longer mine?

For what used to be my lover
The passion of my life
Has changed to something different
She now is, just my wife

j.f. sohn 1/20/98

Mystic Goddess Of Love – Story

The story of this poem is a real mystic mystery. It must have come as a transference from some poor soul in great need, or perhaps it was a hidden longing of my own subconscious mind. I guess we don't always know what it is that we really need to make us content. Whichever, it arrived as a complete message that I wrote fully without changing a word.

I don't recall ever having the image of a mystic anything coming to me in a similar dreamlike sequence, but I have deeply appreciated the sensitivity of its touching message.

As I later read it again, I could strangely visualize and sense the described presence of this Mystic Goddess. It was a beautiful surrealistic image that left me feeling the same event that was told in the message. I asked myself if there was some hidden reason for my receiving this message, or again just the need of some lost soul who wanted to see it in writing or hear my reading of it. This event continues to haunt me.

Mystic Goddess of Love

I had lost all hope, a true love to find
Within this crazy world of mine
In desperation I did say
A prayer to find another way
To ease my wanting, ease the pain
Of love now lost and heart now lame
I looked out far, beyond the stars
Where life began, both theirs and ours
There must be an answer, must be a way

Be it from Heaven or Gods we may say
Give me hope that all chance has not died
Please find me a true love to be at my side

Then out of a moonlit mist that night
Within a dream I sensed the sight
Of a Mystic Goddess, come to me
In response for true love, yet to be
This Goddess of love with sweet caress
Upon my cheek she then did press
I felt her near, I sensed her form
Bathed in moonlight, passing warm
Beyond my reach, beyond my call
She slipped away, away from all
My words of love then buried deep
Within my memories fast asleep
She brought them forth with life and hope
Her past caress did then invoke
A sense of passion I but knew
For lovers real and lovers true
Again I found those feelings lost
A gift she left without a cost

Born by night, in quiet sleep
Beneath a canopy of stars so deep
Into a universe of wanting dreams
That night, she came to me it seems
With visions warm, message real
That true love again I soon would feel

j.f. sohn 2004

Fall Of Life – story

One beautiful fall day while driving through the tranquil countryside, I was taken back by the radiant colors of the leaves on the ground and above them, the dark lace like silhouettes of the tree's bare branches. I said to myself "Rusted leaves and naked limbs of fall". I stopped and made a note of that image and later sat down with my pen and pad and started writing. As I wrote, a secondary vision caught me. The drama of nature's seasonal change of life is much like our own, except that ours only has one season in which to bloom while nature blooms and lives over and over again. When the symbolic frost of our life approaches it is only then that many of us look back and realize that which we now miss and how we could have done things so much better for ourselves and for the one's we cherish.

Fall of Life

Rusted leaves and naked limbs of fall
Awaiting winter's wind and
whited snow to call
A final end to the fruits of spring
Of life and love that this did bring
Of summer days beneath the sun
Of golden fields at harvest run
Of colors rich exploding light
That velvet breeze caressing night
So quickly gone, so greatly missed
In symbolic thought of the life we kissed
We now reflect the moments lost
Those passions rare before the frost
What little time we each did give
To the thing for which we
most should live
Love

j.f. sohn © 1995

Island Free – story

Most of the time we don't openly realize the tensions and burned-out feelings that we live with from day to day. Shattered lives, busy and noisy streets, traffic jambs, insecurities about our work and the future. Bills, bills, bills, Rush, rush, rush – everywhere. I was in that city scene when I was invited to join some friends on a Club Med vacation on the French island of Guadalupe in the Caribbean. Club Med? That's for kids or at least younger men than me – I thought! I looked at the brochures with the beautiful overhanging palm trees and azure blue water and thoughts of young ladies in topless bikinis. I already felt better. It didn't take me long to agree to join my friends. The poem "Island Free" tells the story of my therapy on Guadeloupe.

Island Free

Island free I shall roam
Island far away from home
Beaches warm beneath the sun
A soothing breeze when day is done
Magic moods, magic sounds
Forgotten feelings all abound
Music gay, music dancing
People laughing and romancing
Moonlit shores where lovers walk
Holding hands, no need to talk

Oh island free, oh beauty rare
The joy I feel with you I share
You've purged me of my city thoughts
And troubled days that time
has brought
You've set me free, as you are so
To love and laugh and feel the
glow of life
As only youth did know

j.f. sohn 1986

59

Water's Edge – story

This is not a love poem or love story related to women. This is the love story between human beings and that of nature and the universe. That glorious feeling we experience when we see the many different beauties that they give to us so freely. Too often I have heard the statement that "Beauty is in the eye of the beholder" indicating that beauty is a relative thing as it is experienced by different humans. I believe that this does not apply when speaking of the beauty of nature and the universe above it. I believe that the visual experiences that are depicted in "Water's Edge" are loved and seen as beautiful by all human beings.

Water's Edge

I walked for miles at water's edge
And watched the birds at Dolphin's
Head
I saw the wind in changing course
Dance the sands in mounting force
In swirls and waves of changing light
A choreography of pure delight

And oh that setting sun divine
Each time in colors new I find
Irradiates the western sky
In palettes born of heaven's eye
Its beauty bound reflecting light
Across the sea preceding night
Entrances all who watch in awe
And leaves them blessed for what
they saw

Then followed soon the place to be
Where moon is born from out the sea
And rises slowly high above
To spill on those not yet in love
They walk the shore just hand in hand
Till lunar spell besets its plan
Then suddenly without remorse
That moon and night has set the course
To bond them all forever fast
To that miracle of love that's cast

j.f. sohn96

There are these lonely times when you are faced with the beauty of nature and the one you love is far away. At this time we are already emotionally touched by what we see and we wish that our loved one was there beside us. Life is full of these magic moments that cause us to realize the joy we are missing by not having that constant companion at our side. So many stories are written of the bonding that happens between two people as they stroll the water's edge at sunset.

A moment at sunset

Alone, I sadly walked to
the water's edge and patiently
waited for the sun to hide its
glowing face behind the clouded
mist of approaching night.
A beautiful sunset, with feathery
drifting white clouds decorating
the darkening sky. The breeze was
light but tenderly loving as it
caressed the bare skin of my
arms. I could but think of you
and how it would be if we were
there together, drifting into the
night, when the stars would
cover the heavens and the sound
of waves would wash away
all our cares. It was a beautiful
thought. Maybe someday.

j.f. sohn 2003

This is a simple story. It was the month of December. Mentally not a tempting time to take a walk down to the water's edge of Calibogue Sound and head toward the ocean side of the Island, but it was warm enough with a sweater and jacket. It was a bit more breezy along the water but quite comfortable. I didn't really have a plan of going toward the ocean but I hadn't done that trek for some time and anyway I needed the exercise. It wasn't until I was at the curve of the beach that leads to the ocean that I looked out across the water. There I witnessed one of those extra beautiful phenomena of nature, when wind, sun and sea are perfectly choreographed together. This scene was the inspiration for "Crystal Butterflies". I composed the poem as I walked back along the shore. Too often we stay in the drab comfort of our winter shelters and miss the miracles of beauty that nature so graciously provides. I'm so glad that I took that walk.

Crystal Butterflies

Today I walked the water's edge
With cooling breeze about my head
That caused my cheeks a rosy red
The sun was bright, the sand pristine
As tide retreated from the scene
Exposing shells and other creatures
just as well
I strolled beyond the tranquil shore
Where one can hear the ocean's roar
Around the curve where sound meets sea
A change of scene that pleases me
For out as far as I could see
Across the waters, sunlit bright
O'er rippled sea reflecting light
There did appear in faint disguise
A million crystal butterflies
Beauty dancing there for me
And twinkling brightly on the sea

j.f. sohn 12/02

A Special English Day - The story

Summer 1993 _ I was invited to visit with a friend who was a guest of the owner of a Scottish Castle that had been beautifully renovated. I flew to Manchester, England and rented a car for my trip north. I had not driven through this part of England before and had not made any plans for what paths I would take or of what things to see. I decided to just wing it and discover things as I went along toward Scotland. Actually I find that surprise discoveries of beauty on my own or with a special lady to be highly more stimulating than any pointed out on a guided tour. This was especially true this special day. I did not write the poem until I returned to the States, but the memory was so profound that I had no trouble with it. The special event of that day was one of those that could lead you to believe that you had seen the ultimate beauty of nature that bordered on being a glimpse of heaven. A learned friend of mine who read the poem called it an Epiphany. When finished, I sent a copy to Prince Charles. It was received by him with much appreciation

A Special English Day

Through English countryside I roamed, without
a chart or compass homed.
On twisting roads, by hills of gold, through
village quaint and village old

Passed fertile fields, in vibrant hues of green,
from dark to light, as sunlight beamed from
out between, a gray and clouded sky

In contrast high, the fields above were colors all anew
In stripes of orange, mauve and yellow green with other
accents in between. Diminishing out along the scene in
shades of grayish blue

Then on ahead were sparkling lakes, with ducks
and swans to decorate the quiet water view

And in the woods of forest green, with gentle fern as
floor I sighted soon a single deer and quickly searched
for more

Out again, along the dale, tranquil sheep did graze. And
a hundred dots of white and black on distant canvas
played

And oh those ancient castles tall, with battered walls and
tales within their keep. I yearned to learn their secrets
soon and all their history reap

What setting right for fairy tales and stories yet to learn,
of knights and kings and Robin Hood my childish
thoughts did turn

Cont.

How pleased I was in heart and mind this aesthetic kind of day. What more in England's loveliness could ever come my way?

Then, suddenly, I beheld a view that set my skin to chill. A field of unknown source did blaze, like an electric yellow hill

Framed in darkened trees of bluish green and rows of stone made walls, this intensive scene of beauty bloomed, then suddenly did fall

A kaleidoscope of nature's light, a magic scene in time. So beautiful she shone for me that moment she was mine

No picture seen on postcard views, in books or photos lent. No castle still or scene composed by human hand or bent

Oh, how lucky I to be there then, that magic place and time, for ne'er again will one ever see a landscape so divine

And at the end, when all was gray and the chills had passed away. I tried so hard to find the words but only thought to say

Oh God, thank you for today!
Cont.

Then later on in still repose, I sat and thought
in words composed, that better told my feelings
of, that special English day

You have read it now as it was then but I add
below another end that later came to mind
A truthful fact we oft ignore or simply never find

Were I possessed of wealth and fame,
"a member of the club"
Had I the use of magic wand or genie's
lamp to rub
Had I of all the power known, that comes
to Duke or King
Or had I of all the blessings of the one with
Papal ring
These all above, that place and time,
would nothing mean to be
For the givings of that special day,
were given to me - absolutely free

© Jacques F. Sohn 1993

Castle Dunderave - story

This is the follow up to "A Special English Day". It is the short poetic story of my haunting visit to that mystic Scottish castle I was invited to. I was so taken by that short visit that I wrote this poem in its remembrance. A copy of this poem is now framed and displayed in the castle's Grand Hall along with photos I had taken on a rare clear and beautiful day.

Castle Dunderave

What pleasures deep I did incur
while two days spent exploring her
A castle old with history deep
in Scottish hills, where she does sleep
beside a Loch, that in the morn
does glisten bright reflections
Born of morning mist, mirrored
light of distant shore and parting
birds in flight
What peace I felt, what thoughts did
flow of all the past I did not know
Too quick the hours, too short the stay,
I must again, I must some day,
return to that mystic Castle Dunderave

j.f. sohn 1993

Solemn Thoughts

9/11- Story

For several years I had always made original colorful combined art and poem Christmas cards. I always tried to make them joyful with the cheer and spirit of Christmas time. 2001 was an exception. I couldn't think of anything joyful that year. I could only write a message of sorrow and encouragement.

9/11

This season's card I could not do
With art and poem to help us through
These days of war and homeland strife
Our loss of work, our saddened life
With friends and those we did not know
Who bore the worst from foreign foe

I tried to find an image bright
To overcome this saddened plight
But none would come and never might
Till peace is real and not in flight

So bear with me as I bid you well
That peace will come and soon dispel
The veil of darkness that did lay
Upon us all that fateful day

j.f. sohn 2001

Peace

Peace is fertilized by the blood
of the innocent.

j.f. sohn 2001

Hero Brave

Oh hero brave
Who lies here now in hallowed grave
Forget we not for which you died
Forget we not of those who cried
Forget we not the price you paid
To keep us free and unafraid
Forget we not of all like you
Who from which our harvest grew
Forget we not in solemn thought
The time of peace that you had brought

j.f. sohn

Hope And Reality
Yugoslavia 6/20/92

Perchance the Gods will give us life
In balance for the pain
Perchance we all can live in peace
With shelter from the rain
Perchance we all will learn to love
And cast the hate away
Perchance we'll find that better world
Perchance, but not today

j.f. sohn 92

T'was a cold winters night
Neath a full moonlight
On a snowy Christmas eve
Near all were inside
With a drink to imbibe
And none in a hurry to leave

While high on the roof
Sat this cat so aloof
Awaiting a friend to arrive
For each year on this day
Came that friend and his sleigh
With catnip for cats to revive

So to all you dear cats be you
inside or out
Having your sip or a nip
I bid you all well and a joyous Noel
May the new year to all be a trip

j.f. sohn   96

74

Oh Christmas lights that twinkle
bright in colors wide array
What joy you bring as carolers
sing this merry Holiday
You adorn the roofs by reindeer
hoofs and light up Santa's sleigh
You wind around the lampposts,
encircle every tree
You frame near every widow
and door that we can see
You dot the city corners with
snowflakes brilliant white
You fill our hearts with joyous
love this Holy Christmas night

'Tis Christmas Eve on Hilton Head
The little ones have gone to bed
Some sleep they may till
Christmas day
When all their joy will bound
From sight of presents bright
and wrapped
And others to be found
The wrappings fly and voices cry
In cheers of shear delight
Oh wow - Oh gee - and one yippee
It's such a pleasant sight to see
Their happiness, their joy, their youth
Their innocence, their simple truth
If only we as adults be as easily
to find, again the joy and kind of love
Once Christmas brought to mind

j.f. sohn

A tree for Christmas Eve

Oh Christmas tree, Oh Christmas tree
How hard it is to shop for thee
Go out all day in snow and rain
In search of thee is such a pain
From shop to shop and lot to lot
This one last day is all I've got
To find the tree that satisfies
Those anxious little hopeful eyes
This one's too thin, that one's too fat
Oh perfect tree where are you at
Then just when weriness arrives
And thoughts I had to compromise
There came a call from out a shed
I'm here, I'm here - All bound, unspread
Please cut me loose, extend my boughs
I'll earn for you those Christmas vows
And sure enough, when she was dressed
This hidden tree was beauty blessed
The perfect shape and height I sought
With scent of pine, my breath she caught
How lucky I and lucky she
For no more days were left to see
And no more days for her to be
This beauty perfect Christmas Tree

j.f. sohn 98

La Fin

Alas an end to poetic thoughts
Issues of love and issues of
life
Forever they've been and forever they'll be.
No change can we cause
No change will we see.
So God bless you all whatever your strife
May you find joy in living and love in your life

Jacques F. Sohn 2004

Index of Poems By Page No.